ETERNAL LIGHT

Other Works by Jason Shinder:

Anthologies

DIVIDED LIGHT: Father & Son Poems

FIRST LIGHT: Mother & Son Poems

MORE LIGHT: Father & Daughter Poems

Poetry

EVERY ROOM WE EVER SLEPT IN

Audiocassettes

THE ESSENTIAL JOHN KEATS
with Philip Levine

THE ESSENTIAL WILLIAM BLAKE
with Stanley Kunitz

THE ESSENTIAL JOHN DONNE
with Amy Clampitt

THE ESSENTIAL LORD BYRON
with Paul Muldoon

ETERNAL LIGHT

Grandparent Poems

A Twentieth-Century American Selection

EDITED BY JASON SHINDER

A Harvest Original

Harcourt Brace & Company

San Diego   New York   London

Requests for permission to make copies of any part of the work should
be mailed to: Permissions Department, Harcourt Brace & Company,
6277 Sea Harbor Drive, Orlando, Florida 32887-6777.

The epigraph is excerpted from "Canto LXXXI,"
from *The Cantos of Ezra Pound*. Copyright 1948 by Ezra Pound.
Reprinted by permission of New Directions Publishing Corporation.

Library of Congress Cataloging-in-Publication Data
Eternal light: grandparent poems: a twentieth-century American selection/
edited by Jason Shinder.
p.   cm.
"A Harvest original."
ISBN 0-15-600099-7
1. Grandparents—Poetry.   2. American poetry—20th century.
I. Shinder, Jason, 1955–
PS595.G75E86   1994
811'.540803520432—dc20   94-8749

Text set in Perpetua
Designed by Camilla Filancia
Printed in the United States of America
First edition   A B C D E

In memory of
my grandmother
FANNY SHINDER
1884 – 1991

What thou lovest well remains,

       the rest is dross

What thou lov'st well shall not be reft from thee

What thou lov'st well is thy true heritage

          EZRA POUND

Contents

Introduction

One of the things I loved about my paternal grandmother, Fanny, is that she could always be counted on to say the same things every time I visited her:

You should only be happy and healthy and live a long life.
You should have many blessings from your children.
Are you sure you're making a living?
Is she Jewish?

When she said these things, she had a habit of taking my hands into her hands and squeezing them, with a pleased, satisfied expression on her face. The ritual was urgent, intense, and, for lack of a better word, loving.

These lines were often delivered by my grandmother while we sat in the small yellow kitchen of her fifty-year-old apartment in Brooklyn.

We always ate the same thing we ate the previous time I visited her—a potato wrapped in lettuce and a bowl of broth brimming with sliced chicken left over from the chicken she cooked the night before for herself and her friend Sophie.

There was a handkerchief she carried from day to day, week to week, which was visible underneath the sleeve covering her left arm. She often pulled at the handkerchief, as though wanting something from herself that she didn't have.

Ten, twenty times, I would tell her about my life—this book, this job, this trip.

As she listened, her hands waved back and forth across the table.

"A little this. A little that. So how's mother?"

I always wondered what she felt like when her husband, Max, died so early in their marriage, leaving her with three children to raise alone.

After his death, she learned to be a seamstress, and

spent a great deal of her life at a local factory—sixteen hours a day, seven days a week, fifty-two weeks a year, one or two pennies per button.

She achieved no small amount of joy and success for herself and her family. Yet her happiness was punctuated by acute feelings of anger and sadness for never having enough—enough money, enough clothes, enough furniture, enough time. And she grieved, sometimes openly, for having to live without a husband. Later, when my father died at the age of fifty-one, she grieved for him more privately but no less intensely.

She could never understand why, if she worked so hard so long, and prayed so often for everyone but herself, that there would not be more joy.

At the end of my visits, she would always say: "Don't drive fast."

I would lean my lips upon the dry lips of her small, wrinkled face. I could smell a sourness at the back of her throat, as though rising from all the disappointments of her life.

"Go. You should be healthy and happy . . ."

She opened her mouth and smiled just enough for me to notice.

It is a smile that carried me through the grief I experienced after her death. It is a smile that I often recall during moments of both pleasure and difficulty.

Eternal Light is the first anthology to present poems exclusively by American poets on grandparents. The poems are arranged chronologically so the reader may trace the development of the grandchild-grandparent theme in twentieth-century American poetry.

Many of this century's poems about grandparents were written about the death of a grandmother or grandfather or after the death of a grandparent. When I asked several poets why they did not write about their grandparents while they were living, they often expressed the difficulty of writing about the relationship while experiencing the entanglements that surface from being an active participant.

As a result, many of the poems in this collection were written from the standpoint of looking back and convey a sense of longing for a grandparent no longer present. Yet within this context of longing, the anthologized poems celebrate the work, love, humor, wisdom, disappointments, and joys of grandparents and their relationships with grandchildren.

I have tried to select poems that illuminate most directly and originally the life of grandparents as well as the grandchild-grandparent relationship. I was also drawn to poems that moved beyond the subject of grandchild-grandparent relationships and offered a strong quality of affection and a sense of awareness about the self and of being alive. (As a point of interest, the anthology begins with the rarely anthologized "first version" of William Carlos Williams's well-loved poem to his grandmother, in addition to the final version of the same poem.)

I am grateful to the many poets whose work appears in this collection. I am also grateful to the many people who provided new insights into the poems I was considering, and to the people who brought poems to my attention. Thanks to Loren Segan for her diligent permissions work and her commitment to other aspects of this book.

Thanks, especially, to Ruth Greenstein, editor at Harcourt Brace. Without her unwavering support and invaluable insights, this anthology—and the other anthologies in this series—would not be here.

ETERNAL LIGHT

William Carlos Williams

LAST WORDS
OF MY GRANDMOTHER
[first version]

She stayed over after
the summer people had gone
at her little shack
on the shore, an old woman

impossible to get on with
unless you left her alone
with her things—among them
the young grandson, nineteen

whom she had raised.
He endured her because
he was too lazy to work
too lazy to think and

had a soft spot for her
in his bright heart, also a
moustache, a girl, bed
and board out of the old lady

the sea before him
and a ukulele—The two
had remained on and on
into the cold weather.

Thanksgiving day
after the heavy dinner
at a good neighbor's table
Death touched the old lady

in her head—Home she must
go leaning heavily on the
boy who put her to bed and
gave her what she wanted—

water and Mother Eddy's
Science and Health and
forgot her for other things.
But she began to rave in the night.

In the morning after frying
an egg for her
he combed his whiskers
picked his pimples

and got busy with
a telegram for help—
Gimme something to eat
Gimme something to eat

I'm starving
they're starving me
was all I got out of
the dazed old woman

There were some dirty plates
and a glass of milk
beside her on a small table
near her stinking bed

Wrinkled and nearly blind
she lay and snored
rousing to cry
with anger in her tones—

They're starving me—
You won't move me

I'm all right—I won't go
to the hospital. No, no, no

Give me something to eat!—
Let me take you
to the hospital, I said,
and after you are well

you can do as you please—
She smiled her old smile:
Yes, you do what you please
first then I can do what I please—

Oh, oh, oh, she cried
as the ambulance men lifted her
to their stretcher on the floor—
Is this what you call

making me comfortable?—
Now her mind was clear
Oh you think you're awfully
smart, you young people,

she said to us, but I'll tell
you you don't know
anything—Then we started.
On the way

we passed a long row
of elms, she looked
a long while out of the
ambulance window and said—

What are all those
fuzzy looking things out there?
Trees? Well, I'm
tired of them.

William Carlos Williams

THE LAST WORDS OF
MY ENGLISH GRANDMOTHER

There were some dirty plates
and a glass of milk
beside her on a small table
near the rank, disheveled bed—

Wrinkled and nearly blind
she lay and snored
rousing with anger in her tones
to cry for food,

Gimme something to eat—
They're starving me—
I'm all right I won't go
to the hospital. No, no, no

Give me something to eat
Let me take you
to the hospital, I said
and after you are well

you can do as you please.
She smiled, Yes
you do what you please first
then I can do what I please—

Oh, oh, oh! she cried
as the ambulance men lifted
her to the stretcher—
Is this what you call

making me comfortable?
By now her mind was clear—

Oh you think you're smart
you young people,

she said, but I'll tell you
you don't know anything.
Then we started.
On the way

we passed a long row
of elms. She looked at them
awhile out of
the ambulance window and said,

What are all those
fuzzy-looking things out there?
Trees? Well, I'm tired
of them and rolled her head away.

Mark Van Doren

SLEEP, GRANDMOTHER

Sleep, grandmother, sleep.
The rocking chair is ready to go,
And harness bells are hung in a row
As once you heard them
In soft snow.

Sleep, grandmother, sleep.
Your sons are little and silly again;
Your daughters are five and seven and ten;
And he that is gone
Was not gone then.

Sleep, grandmother, sleep.
The sleigh comes out of the winter woods
And carries you all in boots and hoods
To town for candy
And white dress goods.

Sleep, grandmother, sleep.
The rocking chair is old as the floor,
But there he nods, at the noisy door,
For you to be dancing
One dance more.

MY GRANDMOTHER'S
LOVE LETTERS

There are no stars to-night
But those of memory.
Yet how much room for memory there is
In the loose girdle of soft rain.

There is even room enough
For the letters of my mother's mother,
Elizabeth,
That have been pressed so long
Into a corner of the roof
That they are brown and soft,
And liable to melt as snow.

Over the greatness of such space
Steps must be gentle.
It is all hung by an invisible white hair.
It trembles as birch limbs webbing the air.

And I ask myself:

"Are your fingers long enough to play
Old keys that are but echoes:
Is the silence strong enough
To carry back the music to its source
And back to you again
As though to her?"

Yet I would lead my grandmother by the hand
Through much of what she would not understand;
And so I stumble. And the rain continues on the roof
With such a sound of gently pitying laughter.

Lorine Niedecker

GRANDFATHER

Grandfather
 advised me:
   Learn a trade.
I learned
  to sit at desk
   and condense.
No layoff
  from this
   condensery.

Louise McNeill

GRANNY SAUNDERS

Her ministration was to heal
With pungent herb and bitter peel.
Up in the drying loft she hung
Horehound and sage and blacksnake-tongue,
Wild cherry, spicebush, "penny rorrel,"
Blue monkshood, ginseng, sour sorrel,
Thin twisted stalks, sharp jimsonweeds,
Bloody percoons, hot mustard seeds,
And meadow docks—both broad and narrow,
Rough boneset, golden thread, and yarrow,
Field balsam, catnip, dittany,
All to be simmered down to tea.

All to be brewed for aches and ills—
Red pepper pods for croup and chills;
Spearmint for phthisic; flax for pain;
Horseradish roots for bruise or sprain;
And for uncertain maladies
The northwest bark of dogwood trees.

Kenneth Patchen

FOR THE MOTHER OF
MY MOTHER'S MOTHER

Wind. Flower. Pretty village.
1847.

This is the autumn, Jenny.
Leaves scratch
The lowest star.
Green are the leaves, Jenny.

Pleasure in a warm young body . . .

Dogs snap
At the sullen moon.
Cruel are the dogs, Jenny.
They do their crazysad love
Over your sleeping face.
Snow. Rain. A bad world.

Jenny, my darling Jenny . . .
Black are the leaves that fall
On your grave.

MANNERS

for a Child of 1918

My grandfather said to me
as we sat on the wagon seat,
"Be sure to remember to always
speak to everyone you meet."

We met a stranger on foot.
My grandfather's whip tapped his hat.
"Good day, sir. Good day. A fine day."
And I said it and bowed where I sat.

Then we overtook a boy we knew
with his big pet crow on his shoulder.
"Always offer everyone a ride;
don't forget that when you get older,"

my grandfather said. So Willy
climbed up with us, but the crow
gave a "Caw!" and flew off. I was worried.
How would he know where to go?

But he flew a little way at a time
from fence post to fence post, ahead;
and when Willy whistled he answered.
"A fine bird," my grandfather said,

"and he's well brought up. See, he answers
nicely when he's spoken to.
Man or beast, that's good manners.
Be sure that you both always do."

When automobiles went by,
the dust hid the people's faces,
but we shouted "Good day! Good day!
Fine day!" at the top of our voices.

Karl Shapiro

MY GRANDMOTHER

My grandmother moves to my mind in context of sorrow
And, as if apprehensive of near death, in black;
Whether erect in chair, her dry and corded throat harangued
    by grief,
Or at ragged book bent in Hebrew prayer,
Or gentle, submissive, and in tears to strangers;
Whether in sunny parlor or back of drawn blinds.

Though time and tongue made any love disparate,
On daguerreotype with classic perspective
Beauty I sigh and soften at is hers.
I pity her life of deaths, the agony of her own,
But most that history moved her through
Stranger lands and many houses,
Taking her exile for granted, confusing
The tongues and tasks of her children's children.

Barbara   Howes

FOR STEWART P. PARK:
1907 – 1976

   A Grandfather Clock
Stands; in humane
Script, morning-glories
Flute out from their heartwood center,
Shape what it was and is.

   The pendulum, a brass pulse,
Goes its reflective, rural way,
Steadying; it leans toward change,
It leans toward years past . . .

   This polished wood
Artifact has had so many days
When eyes looked straight for guidance—
Now the tall paneled form
Looms there, striking our memory,
    But the face is gone.

William Stafford

ONE DAY

Near dawn old boxes in the attic
begin to wake up: "Are you there,
albums?" "How are you,
Aunt Milly's hat?"

In his dim corner Grandfather's
big furry boots begin to creak softly.
What ever happened to his plan
to walk all the way down the Yukon?

Somewhere whispering among folded letters
his whiskery chuckle still lingers,
while Aunt Milly sniffs that she never
really believed any man.

They all stir around for a while,
till full day speaks:
the louder the light is,
the quieter the boxes become.

Later their darkness returns and we
go to sleep. The attic above us moves near.
Some time in the night they wake up
and begin to whisper again.

Margaret   Walker

LINEAGE

My grandmothers were strong.
They followed plows and bent to toil.
They moved through fields sowing seed.
They touched earth and grain grew.
They were full of sturdiness and singing.
My grandmothers were strong.

My grandmothers are full of memories
Smelling of soap and onions and wet clay
With veins rolling roughly over quick hands
They have many clean words to say.
My grandmothers were strong.
Why am I not as they?

R o b e r t   L o w e l l

G R A N D P A R E N T S

They're altogether otherworldly now,
those adults champing for their ritual Friday spin
to pharmacist and five-and-ten in Brockton.
Back in my throw-away and shaggy span
of adolescence, Grandpa still waves his stick
like a policeman;
Grandmother, like a Mohammedan, still wears her thick
lavender mourning and touring veil;
the Pierce Arrow clears its throat in a horse-stall.
Then the dry road dust rises to whiten
the fatigued elm leaves—
the nineteenth century, tired of children, is gone.
They're all gone into a world of light; the farm's my own.

The farm's my own!
Back there alone,
I keep indoors, and spoil another season.
I hear the rattley little country gramophone
racking its five foot horn:
"O Summer Time!"
Even at noon here the formidable
Ancien Régime still keeps nature at a distance. Five
green shaded light bulbs spider the billiards-table;
no field is greener than its cloth,
where Grandpa, dipping sugar for us both,
once spilled his demitasse.
His favorite ball, the number three,
still hides the coffee stain.

Never again
to walk there, chalk our cues,
insist on shooting for us both.

Grandpa! Have me, hold me, cherish me!
Tears smut my fingers. There
half my life-lease later,
I hold an *Illustrated London News*—;
disloyal still,
I doodle handlebar
mustaches on the last Russian Czar.

Gwendolyn Brooks

from CHILDREN COMING HOME

Novelle/My Grandmother Is Waiting for Me to Come Home

My Grandmother is waiting for me to come home.
We live with walnuts and apples
in a one-room kitchenette above The
Some Day Liquor Gardens.

My Grandmother sits in a red rocking chair
waiting for me
to open the door with my key.

She is Black and glossy like coal.

We eat walnuts and apples,
drink root beer in cups that are broken,
above The
Some Day Liquor Gardens.

I love my Grandmother.
She is wonderful to behold
with the glossy of her coal-colored skin.
She is warm wide and long.
She laughs and she Lingers.

Marie Ponsot

AMONG   WOMEN

What women wander?
Not many. All. A few.
Most would, now & then,
& no wonder.
Some, and I'm one,

Wander sitting still.
My small grandmother
Bought from every peddler
Less for the ribbons and lace
Than for their scent
Of sleep where you will,
Walk out when you want, choose
Your bread and your company.

She warned me, "Have nothing to lose."

She looked fragile but had
High blood, runner's ankles,
Could endure, endure.
She loved her rooted garden, her
Grand children, her once
Wild once young man.
Women wander
As best they can.

Louis Simpson

A STORY ABOUT
CHICKEN SOUP

In my grandmother's house there was always chicken soup
And talk of the old country—mud and boards,
Poverty,
The snow falling down the necks of lovers.

Now and then, out of her savings
She sent them a dowry. Imagine
The rice-powdered faces!
And the smell of the bride, like chicken soup.

But the Germans killed them.
I know it's in bad taste to say it,
But it's true. The Germans killed them all.

. . .

In the ruins of Berchtesgaden
A child with yellow hair
Ran out of a doorway.

A German girl-child—
Cuckoo, all skin and bones—
Not even enough to make chicken soup.
She sat by the stream and smiled.

Then as we splashed in the sun
She laughed at us.
We had killed her mechanical brothers,
So we forgave her.

. . .

The sun is shining.
The shadows of the lovers have disappeared.
They are all eyes; they have some demand on me—
They want me to be more serious than I want to be.

They want me to stick in their mudhole
Where no one is elegant.
They want me to wear old clothes,
They want me to be poor, to sleep in a room with many
    others—

Not to walk in the painted sunshine
To a summer house,
But to live in the tragic world forever.

Donald Justice

THE GRANDFATHERS

Why will they never sleep?
JOHN PEALE BISHOP

Why will they never sleep,
The old ones, the grandfathers?
Always you find them sitting
On ruined porches, deep
In the back country, at dusk,
Hawking and spitting.
They might have sat there forever,
Tapping their sticks,
Peevish, discredited gods.
Ask the lost traveler how,
At road-end, they will fix
You maybe with the cold
Eye of a snake or a bird
And answer not a word,
Only these blank, oracular
Headshakes or headnods.

Stanley Moss

I HAVE COME TO JERUSALEM

I have come to Jerusalem
because I have a right to,
bringing my family who did not come with me,
who never thought I would bring them here.
I carry them as a sleeping child to bed.
Who of them would not forgive me?
I have come to Jerusalem to dream
I found my mother's mother by chance,
white-haired and beautiful, frightened behind a column,
in a large reception room filled with strangers
wearing overcoats. After forty-two years
I had to explain who I was. "I'm Stanley
your grandson." We kissed and hugged and laughed,
she said we were a modern family,
one of the first to ride on trains.
I hadn't seen before how much she looked like
her great, great granddaughter. I remembered
that in her house I thumped her piano,
I saw my first family painting, a garden, by her lost son.
I remembered the smells of her bedroom:
lace-covered pillows, a face-powdered Old Testament.
Then my dead mother and father came into the room.
I showed them whom I'd found and gave everybody
    chocolates,
we spoke of what was new
and they called me only by my secret name.

Robert Creeley

THE TEACHINGS

of my grandmother
who at over eighty
went west from West Acton,
to see a long lost son named
Archie—by Greyhound, my
other uncle, Hap, got the *Globe*
to photograph her, and us—
came back from Riverside, California,
where Archie was—he'd left
at eighteen—and he'd tried,
she told us, to teach her
religion, "at her age"—"as
much a fool as ever"—and
she never spoke of him again.

James Wright

MY GRANDMOTHER'S GHOST

She skimmed the yellow water like a moth,
Trailing her feet across the shallow stream;
She saw the berries, paused and sampled them
Where a slight spider cleaned his narrow tooth.
Light in the air, she fluttered up the path,
So delicate to shun the leaves and damp,
Like some young wife, holding a slender lamp
To find her stray child, or the moon, or both.

Even before she reached the empty house,
She beat her wings ever so lightly, rose,
Followed a bee where apples blew like snow;
And then, forgetting what she wanted there,
Too full of blossom and green light to care,
She hurried to the ground, and slipped below.

W. S. Merwin

GRANDMOTHER WATCHING AT HER WINDOW

There was always the river or the train
Right past the door, and someone might be gone
Come morning. When I was a child I mind
Being held up at a gate to wave
Good-bye, good-bye to I didn't know who,
Gone to the War, and how I cried after.
When I married I did what was right
But I knew even that first night
That he would go. And so shut my soul tight
Behind my mouth, so he could not steal it
When he went. I brought the children up clean
With my needle, taught them that stealing
Is the worst sin; knew if I loved them
They would be taken away, and did my best
But must have loved them anyway
For they slipped through my fingers like stitches.
Because God loves us always, whatever
We do. You can sit all your life in churches
And teach your hands to clutch when you pray
And never weaken, but God loves you so dearly
Just as you are, that nothing you are can stay,
But all the time you keep going away, away.

A d r i e n n e   R i c h

from *G R A N D M O T H E R S*

1. *Mary Gravely Jones*
We had no petnames, no diminutives for you,
always the formal guest under my father's roof:
you were "Grandmother Jones" and you visited rarely.
I see you walking up and down the garden,
restless, southern-accented, reserved, you did not seem
my mother's mother or anyone's grandmother.
You were Mary, widow of William, and no matriarch,
yet smoldering to the end with frustrate life,
ideas nobody listened to, least of all my father.
One summer night you sat with my sister and me
in the wooden glider long after twilight,
holding us there with streams of pent-up words.
You could quote every poet I had ever heard of,
had read *The Opium Eater,* Amiel and Bernard Shaw,
your green eyes looked clenched against opposition.
You married straight out of the convent school,
your background was country, you left an unperformed
typescript of a play about Burr and Hamilton,
you were impotent and brilliant, no one cared
about your mind, you might have ended
elsewhere than in that glider
reciting your unwritten novels to the children.

2. *Hattie Rice Rich*
Your sweetness of soul was a mystery to me,
you who slip-covered chairs, glued broken china,
lived out of a wardrobe trunk in our guestroom
summer and fall, then took the Pullman train
in your darkblue dress and straw hat, to Alabama,
shuttling half-yearly between your son and daughter.
Your sweetness of soul was a convenience for everyone,

how you rose with the birds and children, boiled your
    own egg,
fished for hours on a pier, your umbrella spread,
took the street-car downtown shopping
endlessly for your son's whims, the whims of genius,
kept your accounts in ledgers, wrote letters daily.
All through World War Two the forbidden word
Jewish was barely uttered in your son's house;
your anger flared over inscrutable things.
Once I saw you crouched on the guestroom bed,
knuckles blue-white around the bedpost, sobbing
your one brief memorable scene of rebellion:
you didn't want to go back South that year.
You were never "Grandmother Rich" but "Anana";
you had money of your own but you were homeless,
Hattie, widow of Samuel, and no matriarch,
dispersed among the children and grandchildren.

.   .   .

Elizabeth Cook-Lynn

GRANDFATHER AT
THE INDIAN HEALTH CLINIC

It's cold at last and cautious winds creep
softly into coves along the riverbank. At my insistence
he wears his denim cowboy coat high on his neck; averse to
an unceremonious world, he follows me through
hallways pushing down the easy rage he always has
with me, a youngest child, and smiles.
This morning the lodge is closed to the dance
and he reminds me these are not the men who
raise the bag above the painted marks; for the young
intern from New Jersey he bares his chest
but keeps a scarf tied on his steel-gray braids
and thinks of days that have no turning: he wore
yellow chaps and went as far as Canada to ride
Mad Dog and then came home to drive the Greenwood
    Woman's
cattle to his brother's place,
two hundred miles
along the timber line
the trees were bright
he turned his hat brim down in summer rain.

Now winter's here, he says, in this white lighted place
where lives are sometimes saved by
throwing blankets over spaces where the leaves are brushed
    away
and giving brilliant gourd-shell rattles
to everyone who comes.

Etheridge Knight

THE IDEA OF ANCESTRY

1

Taped to the wall of my cell are 47 pictures: 47 black
faces: my father, mother, grandmothers (1 dead), grand-
fathers (both dead), brothers, sisters, uncles, aunts,
cousins (1st & 2nd), nieces, and nephews. They stare
across the space at me sprawling on my bunk. I know
their dark eyes, they know mine. I know their style,
they know mine. I am all of them, they are all of me;
they are farmers, I am a thief, I am me, they are thee.

I have at one time or another been in love with my mother,
1 grandmother, 2 sisters, 2 aunts (1 went to the asylum),
and 5 cousins. I am now in love with a 7 yr old niece
(she sends me letters written in large block print, and
her picture is the only one that smiles at me).

I have the same name as 1 grandfather, 3 cousins, 3 nephews,
and 1 uncle. The uncle disappeared when he was 15, just took
off and caught a freight (they say). He's discussed each year
when the family has a reunion, he causes uneasiness in
the clan, he is an empty space. My father's mother, who is 93
and who keeps the Family Bible with everybody's birth dates
(and death dates) in it, always mentions him. There is no
place in her Bible for "whereabouts unknown."

2

Each fall the graves of my grandfathers call me, the brown
hills and red gullies of mississippi send out their electric
messages, galvanizing my genes. Last yr / like a salmon quitting
the cold ocean-leaping and bucking up his birthstream / I
hitchhiked my way from L.A. with 16 caps in my pocket and a
monkey on my back. And I almost kicked it with the kinfolks.

I walked barefooted in my grandmother's backyard / I smelled
    the old land and the woods / I sipped cornwhiskey from
    fruit jars with the men / I flirted with the women / I had a
    ball till the caps ran out
and my habit came down. That night I looked at my grandmother
and split / my guts were screaming for junk / but I was almost
contented / I had almost caught up with me.
(The next day in Memphis I cracked a croaker's crib for a fix.)

This yr there is a gray stone wall damming my stream, and when
the falling leaves stir my genes, I pace my cell or flop on
    my bunk and stare at 47 black faces across the space. I am
    all of them, they are all of me, I am me, they are thee,
    and I have no children to float in the space between.

Linda Pastan

GRUDNOW

When he spoke of where he came from,
my grandfather could have been
clearing his throat
of that name, that town
sometimes Poland, sometimes Russia,
the borders pencilled in
with a hand as shaky as his.
He left, I heard him say,
because there was nothing there.

I understood what he meant
when I saw the photograph
of his people standing
against a landscape emptied
of crops and trees, scraped raw
by winter. Everything
was in sepia, as if the brown earth
had stained the faces,
stained even the air.

I would have died there, I think
in childhood maybe
of some fever,
my face pressed for warmth
against a cow with flanks
like those of the great aunts
in the picture. Or later
I would have died of history
like the others, who dug

their stubborn heels into that earth,
heels as hard as the heels

of the bread my grandfather tore
from the loaf at supper. He always
sipped his tea through a cube of sugar
clenched in his teeth, the way
he sipped his life here, noisily,
through all he remembered
that might have been sweet in Grudnow.

Jean Valentine

MY GRANDMOTHER'S WATCH

Your first child was my father,
Old *muti* of Buffalo, little old child heiress,
My black-eyed baby, chain-smoking gold-
Tipped English Ovals in Heaven: your brassy
Churchillian French reduced us all to *mots,*
Even from the hardly troubled, lavendered sheets of your
    deathbed.

I wear your coin-thin red gold watch now, Momma,
Its face benign as the Archduke's, and think of your hours,
And what has gone between us, what is ours.
Tonight, for instance: my tongue is thick with longing:
When the children's visit was over, the cake cleared away,
What possessed your mahogany beasts to stay?

On the night of my eighteenth birthday
You made me a toast, saying I
Was not only good at school, but musical!
Pink-cheeked, black-hearted, shy,
I couldn't even look you in the eye:
They cleared the cake away.

The insanely steady minute-hand sweeps round,
The hours go by. Somebody said
His Viennese grandfather
Sold him his watch on his deathbed.
Did you too?

What can I do?

O Momma, what can I
Do with this gold and crystal that goes by?

Diane di Prima

APRIL FOOL BIRTHDAY POEM
FOR GRANDPA

Today is your
birthday and I have tried
writing these things before,
but now
in the gathering madness, I want to
thank you
for telling me what to expect
for pulling
no punches, back there in that scrubbed Bronx parlor
thank you
for honestly weeping in time to
innumerable heartbreaking
italian operas for
pulling my hair when I
pulled the leaves off the trees so I'd
know how it feels, we are
involved in it now, revolution, up to our
knees and the tide is rising, I embrace
strangers on the street, filled with their love and
mine, the love you told us had to come or we
die, told them all in that Bronx park, me listening in
spring Bronx dusk, breathing stars, so glorious
to me your white hair, your height your fierce
blue eyes, rare among italians, I stood
a ways off, looking up at you, my grandpa
people listened to, I stand

a ways off listening as I pour out soup
young men with light in their faces
at my table, talking love, talking revolution
which is love, spelled backwards, how
you would love us all, would thunder your anarchist wisdom

Colleen McElroy

GRA'MA

Gra'ma was a little bit of a thing,
Full of spirits wandering
From an Alabama plantation to St. Louis.
Three on a match and a hat on the bed
Says the oldest will die.
She told me this at the age of five.
Her skin spoke of Chinese coolies
And overseers. Her face sang
Of Tanzania near Congolese waters,
Crocodiles running rapidly by
Gathering stones as a village screamed
Its death throes. That combination
Got her in the house when she was young;
Scrubbing, serving and suckling
Pink babies. Kept her there
Until 40 acres and a mule
Times a hundred kin freed her
With that long tall man
We came to love as Papa.
Set them near a Georgia swamp,
Pulling half a year's living
From the soil. He moved her north
Where she had a story for every day.
Told me: Listen close, child,
The world and the Lord are both profound.
When Papa died, her stories grew shorter;
She forgot which of those 40 acres
Could be mine or how many mules
You need to pull a plow.
When she finally saw my son,
She said: I guess the mules
Done long since gone.

Lucille Clifton

DAUGHTERS

woman who shines at the head
of my grandmother's bed,
brilliant woman, i like to think
you whispered into her ear
instructions. i like to think
you are the oddness in us,
you are the arrow
that pierced our plain skin
and made us fancy women;
my wild witch gran, my magic mama,
and even these gaudy girls.
i like to think you gave us
extraordinary power and to
protect us, you became the name
we were cautioned to forget.
it is enough,
you must have murmured,
to remember that i was
and that you are. woman, i am
lucille, which stands for light,
daughter of thelma, daughter
of georgia, daughter of
dazzling you.

Sandra M. Gilbert

MY GRANDMOTHER IN PARIS

Paris. 1900. A sky of corrugated iron. Snow and mud.
Beggars like heaps of debris on street corners.
Women with pink cheeks melting in doorways.
Splashes of laughter, church bells, creaking boots.
Puccini's Paris, Paris of *La Bohème,* Paris
of garrets and prisons, Paris of sweet fevers, Paris

of phlegm and sweat, ivory breasts, skylights, *opéra:*
Paris of Wagner and Rilke, Paris of delicious
nineteenth-century melancholy, Paris where streetlights
glisten through the winter twilight
like pomegranates in hell.
                         Twilight.

My grandmother walks in the Bois de Boulogne
under frosted chestnuts. She's twelve years old,
a roundfaced girl just come from Russia,
her hair in skinny braids
like strange embroidery around her head.
She's on her way to the house of the Russian priest

where her mother cooks and cleans
but she watches, wondering, as carriages plunge
through the slush of the Bois, their lamps
leaping like goblin heads, their blanketed horses
clopping docile as cows through all the Paris noise.
Baudelaire is dead, Rimbaud dead in Africa, Gertrude Stein

thinking in Baltimore, Picasso painting in Barcelona.
My grandmother has learned three words of French:
allo, comment, combien. Amedée, the boy she's
going to marry four years from now,

is in Nice with his sister Eugénie,
who will die next year at nineteen,

and his sister Rosette, who will die at forty.
My grandmother is still tired from last week.
She stops to sit on a low wall beside the road
and begins to shape a tiny angel out of crumbs of snow.
From a passing *fiacre* a young clerk off to the *opéra*
sees her round pink face suspended like a small balloon

in the blue air.
                    What is she thinking
as she pats a cold celestial head and frozen wings?
Is she remembering the awful trainride
across Europe, the bonfires at the Polish border, the shouts
as the engine chuffed into Berlin? No. She rises,

makes her angel into a snowball and tosses it at a tree.
She's thinking of Russia, of her grandmother back in the room
in Rostov-on-the-Don, of the ice like silver on the river
all winter and long into spring, of the black fields
outside town and the old stories of Baba Yaga and the tales
she has also heard of the redhaired cossack

said to be her own father.
                    She walks faster.
It's late and cold. Her mother will worry.
The fat priest will be cross. Paris
grows around her like an enigmatic alphabet.
Even the trees are different here. No firs, no birches!
As she walks, Baba Yaga's house on chicken legs
steps delicately away across snowy meadows

and her father the cossack, with his furry animal head,
      fierce teeth
                    red beard,
gallops into glacial distances.

(Does she suspect that from now on
she'll never really know any language again?)

Tomorrow the priest will be sixty. To celebrate
he'll buy a Swiss cane at the Galéries Lafayette.
                                    In seventy years
my grandmother will twirl that cane and dance a twostep
among the eucalyptuses above San Francisco Bay,
singing me the song about the lost princess of the Volga

while, far below, the cold Pacific
glitters like an ice field.

Michael S. Harper

GRANDFATHER

In 1915 my grandfather's
neighbors surrounded his house
near the dayline he ran
on the Hudson
in Catskill, NY
and thought they'd burn
his family out
in a movie they'd just seen
and be rid of his kind:
the death of a lone black
family is *the Birth*
of a Nation,
or so they thought.
His 5'4" waiter gait
quenched the white jacket smile
he'd brought back from watered
polish of my father
on the turning seats,
and he asked his neighbors
up on his thatched porch
for the first blossom of fire
that would burn him down.
They went away, his nation,
spittooning their torched necks
in the shadows of the riverboat
they'd seen, posse decomposing;
and I see him on Sutter
with white bag from your
restaurant, challenged by his first
grandson to a foot-race
he will win in white clothes.

I see him as he buys galoshes
for his railed yard near Mineo's
metal shop, where roses jump
as the el circles his house
toward Brooklyn, where his rain fell;
and I see cigar smoke in his eyes,
chocolate Madison Square Garden chews
he breaks on his set teeth,
stitched up after cancer,
the great white nation immovable
as his weight wilts
and he is on a porch
that won't hold my arms,
or the legs of the race run
forwards, or the film
played backwards on his grandson's eyes.

Toi   Derricotte

THE   WEAKNESS

That time my grandmother dragged me
through the perfume aisles at Saks, she held me up
by my arm, hissing, "Stand up,"
through clenched teeth, her eyes
bright as a dog's
cornered in the light.
She said it over and over,
as if she were Jesus,
and I were dead. She had been
solid as a tree,
a fur around her neck, a
light-skinned matron whose car was parked, who walked
      on swirling
marble and passed through
brass openings—in 1945.
There was not even a black
elevator operator at Saks.
The saleswoman had brought velvet
leggings to lace me in, and cooed,
as if in the service of all grandmothers.
My grandmother had smiled, but not
hungrily, not like my mother
who hated them, but wanted to please,
and they had smiled back, as if
they were wearing wooden collars.
When my legs gave out, my grandmother
dragged me up and held me like God
holds saints by the
roots of the hair. I begged her
to believe I couldn't help it. Stumbling,
her face white
with sweat, she pushed me through the crowd, rushing

away from those eyes
that saw through
her clothes, under
her skin, all the way down
to the transparent
genes confessing.

Sharon Olds

BIRTHDAY POEM
FOR MY GRANDMOTHER

for L.B.M.C., 1890–1975

I stood on the porch tonight—   which way do we
face to talk to the dead?   I thought of the
new rose,   and went out over the
grey lawn—   things really
have no color at night.   I descended
the stone steps,   as if to the place where one
speaks to the dead.   The rose stood
half-uncurled,   glowing white in the
black air.   Later I remembered
your birthday.   You would have been ninety and getting
roses from me.   Are the dead there
if we do not speak to them?   When I came to see you
you were always sitting   quietly in the chair,
not knitting,   because of the arthritis,
not reading,   because of the blindness,
just sitting.   I never knew how you
did it or what you were thinking.   Now I
sometimes sit on the porch,   waiting,
trying to feel you there like the colors of the
flowers in the dark.

Louise Glück

from *DEDICATION TO HUNGER*
2 / GRANDMOTHER

"Often I would stand at the window—
your grandfather
was a young man then—
waiting, in the early evening."

That is what marriage is.
I watch the tiny figure
changing to a man
as he moves toward her;
the last light rings in his hair.
I do not question
their happiness. And he rushes in
with his young man's hunger,
so proud to have taught her that:
his kiss would have been
clearly tender—

Of course, of course. Except
it might as well have been
his hand over her mouth.

L E G A C I E S

her grandmother called her from the playground
 "yes, ma'am"
 "i want chu to learn how to make rolls," said the old
woman proudly
but the little girl didn't want
to learn how because she knew
even if she couldn't say it that
that would mean when the old one died she would be less
dependent on her spirit so
she said
 "i don't want to know how to make no rolls"
with her lips poked out
and the old woman wiped her hands on
her apron saying "lord
 these children"
and neither of them ever
said what they meant
and i guess nobody ever does

James Tate

SUMMER NIGHT

"If you raise canary birds," my grandfather said to me,
"feed them birdseed." Indeed, it is certain disaster
to not give them water as well, I figured out for myself.
And sonic booms will give them a headache, they have no taste

for coffee. "No Zosine," I moaned softly, "No, Zosine."
Long after his death, one man arose to defend his memory.
Unfortunately, that man's character and writings made him
certain to do more harm than good. Brittle stars,

sea lilies, I sit here at the window and gaze back at the waiters
on the kitchen porch of the Chinese restaurant, getting cool
after a hot spell. They don't know how to interpret what
     they see,
dinosaurs two feet long, worms thirty feet long, a one-ton

jellyfish. "Must they not have terrible, cold hearts,"
Zosine again whispered, "to figure out everything like that?
And to go on, day by day, carrying out their scheme."
I longed for the gift to shake loose rain, but only briefly.

Variations, pigments: next door the painted lady and the red
admiral, the spangled fritillary, cannonsmoke and sewing
     machine.
My grandfather also said, "The brightness of the colors is said
to depend upon the emotions of the insect. What a beautiful
     way

to express one's feelings, to be able to flow like melted gold
when one is happy." He obviously did not want to take
his own business seriously, but all the same his voice had
     changed.
The Lion hath not prevailed. To open the book, and to loose

the seven seals thereof (to judge every one according to his
    state):
the wings of the male are velvety black and those of the female
are smoky in color, with a distinct white stigmata spot on
    the tip
of each wing. Common as Tasmanian grasshoppers. Common

task, water. Dreadful fantasies chattered, laughed. Metallic
black, the storm was on the right, path. The race of Edwin
a long, mild, intense glance. Moss animals, labor, hinged
shells. Lake monsters, nobody really knows what to do with
    them.

There is no other name, backboneless. Adults that emerge
during wet weather are frequently darker in color than adults
that emerge during dry weather. Aquatic labor, ribbon-shaped,
coiled. "Nay, Zosine, be quiet," I whispered, "You have
    been dreaming."

"If you are right," said Zosine, "if you are right, if all this
is possible, what are we to do then?"

THE OLD PEOPLE SPEAK
OF DEATH

for Leona Smith, my grandmother

the old people speak of death
frequently now
my grandmother speaks of those now
gone to spirit
now less than bone

they speak of shadows
that graced their days made lovelier
by their wings of light speak of years
& corpses of years of darkness
& of relationships buried
deeper even than residue of bone
gone now beyond hardness
gone now beyond form

they smile now from ingrown roots
of beginnings of those who have left us
& climbed back through the holes the old folks
left in their eyes
for them to enter through

eye walk back now with this poem
through the holes the old folks left in their eyes
for me to enter through walk back to where
eye see them there

the ones that have gone beyond hardness
the ones that have gone beyond form
see them there
darker than where roots began

& lighter than where they go
with their spirits
heavier than stone their memories
sometimes brighter than the flash
of sudden lightning

but green branches will grow
from these roots darker than time
& blacker than even the ashes of nations
sweet flowers will sprout
& wave their love-stroked language
in sun-tongued morning's shadow
the spirit in all our eyes

they have gone now back
to shadow as eye climb back out
from the holes of these old folks eyes
those spirits who sing through this poem
gone now back with their spirits
to fuse with greenness
enter stones & glue their invisible
faces upon the transmigration of earth
nailing winds singing guitar blues
voices through the ribcages
of these days
gone now to where the years run
darker than where roots begin
greener than what they bring

the old people speak of death
frequently now
my grandmother speaks of those now
gone to spirit
now less than bone

Ellen Bryant Voigt

SHORT STORY

My grandfather killed a mule with a hammer,
or maybe with a plank, or a stick, maybe
it was a horse—the story varied
in the telling. If he was planting corn
when it happened, it was a mule, and he was plowing
the upper slope, west of the house, his overalls
stiff to the knees with red dirt, the lines
draped behind his neck.
He must have been glad to rest
when the mule first stopped mid-furrow;
looked back at where he'd come, then down
to the brush along the creek he meant to clear.
No doubt he noticed the hawk's great leisure
over the field, the crows lumped
in the biggest elm on the opposite hill.
After he'd wiped his hatbrim with his sleeve,
he called to the mule as he slapped the line
along its rump, clicked and whistled.

My grandfather was a slight, quiet man,
smaller than most women, smaller
than his wife. Had she been in the yard,
seen him heading toward the pump now,
she'd pump for him a dipper of cold water.
Walking back to the field, past the corncrib,
he took an ear of corn to start the mule,
but the mule was planted. He never cursed
or shouted, only whipped it, the mule
rippling its backside each time
the switch fell, and when that didn't work
whipped it low on its side, where it's tender,
then cross-hatched the welts he'd made already.

The mule went down on one knee,
and that was when he reached for the blown limb,
or walked to the pile of seasoning lumber; or else,
unhooked the plow and took his own time to the shed
to get the hammer.
                              By the time I was born,
he couldn't even lift a stick. He lived
another fifteen years in a chair,
but now he's dead, and so is his son,
who never meant to speak a word against him,
and whom I never asked what his father
was planting and in which field,
and whether it happened before he married,
before his children came in quick succession,
before his wife died of the last one.
And only a few of us are left
who ever heard that story.

Michael Pettit

DRIVING LESSON

for Suzanne

Beside him in the old Ford pickup
that smelled of rope and grease and cattle feed,
sat my sister and I, ten and eight, big
now our grandfather would teach us
that powerful secret, how to drive.
Horizon of high mountain peaks visible
above the blue hood, steering wheel huge
in our hands, pedals at our toe-tips,
we heard his sure voice urge us
Give it gas, give it gas. Over the roar
of the engine our hearts banged
like never before and banged on
furiously in the silence after
we bucked and stalled the truck.
How infinitely empty it then seemed—
windy flat rangeland of silver-green
gramma grass dotted with blooming cactus
and jagged outcrops of red rock, beginnings
of the Sangre de Cristos fifty miles off.
All Guadelupe County, New Mexico,
nothing to hit, and we could not
get the damn thing going. Nothing to hit
was no help. It was not the mechanics
of accelerator and clutch, muscle and bone,
but our sheer unruly spirits
that kept us small with the great desire
to move the world by us, earth and sky
and all the earth and sky contained.
And how hard it was when,
after our grandfather who was a god

said *Let it out slow, slow* time and again
until we did and were at long last rolling
over the earth, his happy little angels,
how hard it was to listen
not to our own thrilled inner voices
saying *Go, go,* but to his saying
the *Good, good* we loved but also
the *Keep it in the ruts* we hated to hear.
How hard to hold to it—
single red vein of a ranch road
running out straight across the mesa,
blood we were bound to follow—
when what we wanted with all our hearts
was to scatter everywhere, everywhere.

Thadious M. Davis

IT'S ALL THE SAME

My Grandmama
dont believe they walked in space:
"In the desert someplace,
Child, where your sense?"
dont believe they traveled to the moon
"On a mountain somewhere,
Child, watch what I say!"

My Grandmama
wont admit there're still Albinos:
"Now we fight for it, they done stopped
stealing our color for sunning oil."
wont admit they let blacks go to Africa:
"What, for this here country to c'lapse?"

On Sunday morning
her old-time preacher preaches the old word:
"And the Sun *do* move!
And the Moon *do* shine!"
And my righteous grandmama,
stronger than a matter-of-fact,
leads the Amen chorus:
"Tell it . . . Tell it . . .
Tell the Gospel Truth, Rev."

THE BEACH AT ST. ANNE'S

i

On visitors' afternoons the old men and women,
the grandfathers and grandmothers,
the brothers and sisters, are wheeled outside.
Two sometimes three rows of them,
blankets over their knees, scarves holding up their heads.
The nurses wheel them past a shock of red maples
to a hill near the sea. They look down
on the endless water which never stops
pushing forward and pulling back. My grandmother
keeps on her lap the maple leaves
I have gathered for her. When she puts her hands
over her ears, I say Yes, the sea is noisy.
And when she puts two fingers into her mouth,
digging under her tongue, I do not resist
the shining string of saliva she winds around my finger.
I put the maple leaves into her hands,
I take her hands between mine and rub them.
I rub the sun into them. And the wind.

ii

The path down to the beach is narrow and brilliant white.
This Sunday afternoon the sea is blowing
back on itself, blue scale over blue scale.
I listen to the clouds gathering in the sky.
I listen to my feet kicking up sand.
Against tide, against wind, three gulls rise
and fall with the waves, drifting toward shore.
I listen to their white heads, their white wings.
I listen until I have to ask the world a favor.
I listen until I have to ask
the world to do this one thing for me.

Because even now I am forgetting, I ask
not to forget. I ask that my hands should not forget.
I ask that my feet should not forget.
Because even now I am forgetting
I ask to stay awake forever
only so that I should not forget
those who are forgetting me
those who are forgetting me and asking to be forgotten.

MEDICINE

Grandma sleeps with
my sick
            grand-
pa so she
can get him
during the night
medicine
to stop
    the pain

        In
    the morning
        clumsily
            I
    wake
        them

Her eyes
look at me
from under-
                neath
his withered
arm

    The
medicine
    is all
        in
her long
    un-
        braided
                hair.

Anne Waldman

JULY 4TH

Wood green. Grandfather built it.
But Grandfather is dead. He puts
down the glassblower's tube to die
a Lutheran. He starts the black
Ford sedan one last time. He wears
working glass spectacles on his
pale face.

Metal holders are spread like
fans on the front of the house
supporting American flags small enough
a child can wave as the boats go by.

O D E

Grandma stuffed her fur coat into the icebox.
God Himself couldn't convince her it wasn't a closet.
"God take me away this minute!" was her favorite Friday
    night prayer.
Nothing made sense, she said. Expect heartburn & bad
    teeth, not sense.
Leave a meat fork in a dairy dish & she'd break the dish
    & bury the fork.
"I spit on this house, on this earth & on God for putting
    me in this life that spits on me night & day," she cried,
    forgetting the barley in barley soup. It wasn't age. She
    believed she was put here to make
one unforgivable mistake after another. Thou shalt be
    disappointed
was God's first law. Her last words were: "Turn off
    the stove
before the house blows up." Listen, I'm thirty-four already
& nothing I do is done well enough. But what if disappointment
is faith & not fate? What if we never wanted anything enough
    to hurt over?
All I can say is spring came this year with such a wallop
the trees are still shaking. Grandma, what do we want
    from them?
What do we want?

Mary   Stuart   Hammond

GRANDMOTHER'S RUG

*32" × 43" rug of useful size, hooked c. 1911 by mountain women
according to a design by the artist Mary Evelyn Kirk. First phase
Cubism of significant original vision. Last completed work. $750.00*
   —INSURANCE APPRAISAL

On days I'm not listening,
when the words escape rebellious as steam
from the snap-bean pot, hustle, answering
only to me, into lines and stanzas,
I kneel on Grandmother's rug come to rest
on a herringbone floor four flights over Manhattan,
and cup my hand around the precise green lobe,
the blood rim of an ear full of yarn sky
floating detached in a divided eternity since 1911—
two years before the Armory Show—and I whisper
into the hooked earth of Virginia, "Hey, Grandmom,
by heavens, I'm doing it." She was so good

in 1912 she came home, Mary Evelyn Kirk,
married Mr. Hammond, who, ever after, called her
Miz Hammond, even in her dreams, she,
who bore him five live children, went to the dances
and Hot Springs, wore blue lace and gardenias,
and never painted again. And yet the artist

traded poems with me like secrets—sonnets, couplets,
villanelles tucked in with birthday checks, saying
hers were not so good—and filled the ballroom attic
with flower containers, collecting hundreds, thousands,
from all the accessible countries, England to China,
in all formalities, earthenware to Lalique,
leaping centuries, Etruscan to Steuben,
mustering them on long rows of tables

like an army of women, their throats and mouths
open in a howl to the eaves. Every morning

she tied a straw hat under her chin,
slipped an ancient egg basket on her arm,
and browsed in the gardens, selecting her palette:
roses and moonwort, dahlias and peonies,
snippets of ivy, boxwood, sorghum—even
kale and eggplant had beauty. Then
she'd climb to the attic, walk up and down
between the tables, studying the containers,
choosing which mouths to give voice to. By eleven,
still lifes supported by frogs and chicken wire,
hidden inside Delft and Limoges and Gallé,
posed on flat lacquer stands in all the rooms,
or waited in a line by the front door for judging,
a few so good, to me they're committed
as oil to canvas, as Manet's *Pinks and Clematis,*
Van Gogh's *Oleanders,* the rest
captured in a steamer trunk of Blue Ribbons,
the way the meadow and the garden
reside in potpourri. Even so, the unused

cerulean blues, the cadmium yellows
entered her bones, crippling her with nagging,
complaints, hypochondria, real arthritis dwarfing her
like the bonsai trees of her Late Period
she sculpted, pruning the roots, pinching
back and wiring shoots and branches until
they were pictures of the wind. So

on the best days, when my ear is full of sky
and the words come so good it feels like 1911
must have felt to her, I like to give her a tickle.
I dance barefoot on her rug, planting red,
harlot toenails first in the scarlet, bourrée,
bourrée into the beige, lopsided earth, holding

on demi-point in the eye that looks like an egg
sunnyside up and fertilized, a couple of tendus
over the ear in the windowpane dividing eternity,
and in the field where color and line connect
two feet off the frontal plane, the mirage
enters my legs, travels into my hips and trunk,
keeping my bones straight and supple, and I sing
loud enough for Roanoke.

Marilyn Nelson Waniek

MY GRANDFATHER
WALKS IN THE WOODS

Somewhere
in the light above the womb,
black trees
and white trees
populate a world.

It is a March landscape,
the only birds around are small
and black.
What do they eat,
sitting in the birches
like warnings?

The branches of the trees
are black and white.
Their race is winter.
They thrive in cold.

There is my grandfather
walking among the trees.
He does not notice
his fingers are cold.
His black felt hat
covers his eyes.

He is knocking on each tree,
listening to their voices
as they answer slowly
deep, deep from their roots.

I am John, he says,
are you my father?

They answer
with voices like wind
blowing away from him.

Bruce Smith

INCUNABULUM: WITH
GRANDMOTHER AT NUZZIE'S

You'll go into it once more. The taproom
without the glow, without the screen door
on the umbilical coil that slams like the pledge
winter or summer or this time
when the Italian Woman,
the bride who wed by mail,
takes her left breast from her shift
as easily as she unwrapped the onion skin promise
from America. Here in the dark,
your eye is the toothless mouth
of her child as it finds milk.

In the brine, in the smoke,
the stammering bar rag in your face
at the rail. You sit down
to the nude above the mirror
with your grandmother. Oh, you love her
and this amber, the silver necks
on the Schenley, the Four Roses—
that's what grandmother likes
in a glass that clicks on her teeth
while the register sings, "Anything, everything."
You've got a pink drink with fruit
and she's proud of your manners,
of the way you can read the epithets of bottles.
You can swivel in your chair
from the nude to the Italian Woman,
from the Woman to the nude.
You're the whirling boy
and the stirring from the belly

is what a shot must do when it empties
into you and the gem of the glass
returns to its gleaming wet O.
Who wanted a body
harder than these shades?
Who wanted to thicken into this?

Carolyn Leilani Lau

from *K O L O H E*

HAKKA GRANDMA IN HAWAI'I

Complaining while washing dishes mother hints that
　"Your father asked my father for my hand in marriage
　in Hawaiian."

　　　　　　　—What did these two *guys* say to each other?
　　　Was it the Chinese or Hawaiian phonemes that
　　　lyricized each other's
　　　greed and passion to inherit instant *ali'i huangdi?*
　　　　　　　　　　　(take a breath!)

　　　Was it a moment of Smithsonian level *Haku-mele?*
Ai ya!　Ai ya　　　Auwe　　*pilikia,*　　auh huh.
　　　(You know *kaona.* You know what they were doing
　　　You know they were up to no good)
　　　Did they graft Chinese concept into Hawaiian
　　　erotica?
　　　　　　　Was it the *mana? aloha?* Or, a matter of
　　　　　　　lust for　　　lust?

　　　How about the issue of *kala, chyan:*
　　　the MONEY.
　　　Did they drink? Must've.

　　　Did daddy promise not to be Hawaiian to gain his
　　　bride?
　　　Did grandpa see a sanction to wiggle his hopes and
　　　serenade his beautiful young wife at any possible
　　　occasion?
Pretty pretty
grandma. Petal skin beauty mark lilting above the
　　　curve of her left lip nearly bald

from every day pulling the hair into the black flower.
Knock your wind out, body goes
limp when you see the photo of her.
Something inside her body   pulls your nose up to her
        picture   stirs your logic
"So so pretty   even after twelve kids."
        My grandma.
Mona Lisa mouth
butterfly eyes.   Bones.
No stereotype doctor or teacher. Poor. A slave all her
        life. No agenda.
That smile: Look, you can tell.
                                My 99%9999 Han man
                        only dreams that he had grandpa's luck.

        Sweet young grandma who despised grandpa when
he did the hula and flirted in Hawaiian.

Nice grandma who loved me most because

                        (everyone in the family will nod and know)
I was the worst. I *needed* the most love.
I was unpure: white and Hawaiian
I pulled her bun
Tied her in knots to her hospital bed and wound
the bed into a **V** while cheating at Chinese checkers.
I stole her silver dollars and bigass fifty-cent pieces.
I tickled her
When she screamed and threatened, I tickled her
        more.
We rocked and rolled in the cuckoo's nest
feeling like grandpa when occasionally, he turned
        Hawaiian.

Len Roberts

MAKING GALUMPKIS

My grandmother pounds sausage and rice
into small mounds, then unrolls the cabbage
leaves to drown them in the long blue pot brimmed
with tomato sauce. I help her wrap what
we call galumpkis, then watch
her shove the pan into the oven, straighten
to whisper her cooking prayer to the white cross
above the table. While they bake she repeats
the story of my father out in ten degrees
below zero, drinking whiskey with that woman,
my mother, says when they sent him home
from the war he weighed only ninety pounds
and had to lay in bed for a year. In the pantry
she mutters malaria, Marjorie, jungle rot
to the dark pots and pans, then turns,
her voice rising as she clatters the plates
and cup down, tells me to eat. So I do, gulping
five of them at the first serving, unbuckling
my belt in my grandmother's honor, while
behind me she kneels and clicks the beads
of her rosary, rises only to see
if I need more, than taps once, twice, three
times on my forehead, looks me right in the eye
to ask if I'm still behaving.

Jane Kenyon

STAYING AT GRANDMA'S

Sometimes they left me for the day
while they went—what does it matter
where—away. I sat and watched her work
the dough, then turn the white shape
yellow in a buttered bowl.

A coleus, wrong to my eye because its leaves
were red, was rooting on the sill
in a glass filled with water and azure
marbles. I loved to see the sun
pass through the blue.

"You know," she'd say, turning
her straight and handsome back to me,
"that the body is the temple
of the Holy Ghost."

The Holy Ghost, the oh, oh . . . the *uh
oh,* I thought, studying the toe of my new shoe,
and glad she wasn't looking at me.

Soon I'd be back in school. No more mornings
at Grandma's side while she swept the walk
or shook the dust mop by the neck.

If she loved me why did she say that
two women would be grinding at the mill,
that God would come out of the clouds
when they were least expecting him,
choose one to be with him in heaven
and leave the other there alone?

Lawrence Joseph

YOU ONLY EXIST
INSIDE ME

Where Dix Highway ends
long boats tug ore
across a green canal.
In a cafe, Yemenites
cheat at dice
and talk about whores.
You drink coffee,
smoke, remember
a room, a table
that held the weight
of your elbows,
the small notebook
in which you wrote
"our labor put the world on wheels";
one day someone
will find it and think
of thick-lipped buckets,
iron pigs growing
into billets.
Alone, I walk this street
of ice, making this up:
you only exist inside me.
A siren blows.
It is 3:30.
I remember how
I punched the clock.
My legs jerked into full stride
toward a room.

I sat at a table
rubbing my eyes.

I did not feel.
I did not think.

A l a n   C h o n g   L a u

"SUN YAT SEN COMES TO LODI"

for my great grandfather, ou ch' ü-chia

1

SUN YAT SEN COMES TO LODI
grandfather in pinstripes
mouth sporting a toothpick
tells friends, "no sin, no sin,
no sir, no sin to get excited"

mr. yee's four-year-old beaming in a pink meenop
hair's done up in pinktails
sam wo has closed his laundry
only day of the year he would do this
excepting new year's

the good doctor smiles
from a sedan's back seat
cheers resound
delta dust flies

there is the speech
"china will be china again"
this brings tears

not losing a minute
to sip
he tells us all that money buys arms
money drives out manchus

most people understand, there is little hesitation
the new york yankees have not yet won the pennant
it is too early to predict weather or the lucky number

but money is dug from pockets
pulled from cloth bags

when the time comes
he says thank you
a cry of genuine sadness
a rush to take seats for a last picture

photographer tong yee
fumbles underneath a black shroud like a soul leaving body
poses change legs shift position
nobody seems to mind too much
only local banker wong hesitates
meeting the public often, he declines
offering a bigger contribution instead

grandfather sits by the doctor's side
pausing only to doff his hat
remove a coin from the ear
and drop a wet toothpick in a spittoon

2

he is proud of that picture
brown and bent in one corner
the only photo left in the family album
since big sister's marriage

there is also a newspaper clipping
with the headline
"SUN YAT SEN COMES TO LODI"
spread out all in characters
that could be relatives telling a story
or scales of a black bass dripping evidence of water

never having learnt the language
i just have to go by hearsay

TANGO

loose in the brush pines
my grandfather farmed
learned yiddish to better wash windows
the french windows
the sixteen paned windows
the terraced windows
of a restricted town
he made violins of pine
varnished them tuned them
let music carry his daughters
out of the town
away from the farm that
burned down
scrubby pines brush pines
obliterate the ruins of the barn
the pine needles scratch the air
each time my father wipes the
tears from his cheeks
but not from the windows
there were never streaks
on the windows.

M a r k   R u d m a n

M A N N E R S

In late August I walked out to the barn (that's where the
    phone was)
at dusk with Sam to make two phone calls: one to congratulate
a close friend who'd just had a baby, another to let
my mother know I was in Vermont. The light was failing,
but I was wrapped in the soothing odor of dung and
the sound of horses stamping and snorting, and Sam was tying
himself to the corral gate a few feet away with tack.
I couldn't get him to come to the phone and this provoked
a mild tirade. My mother wanted to know if I could
take Sam to restaurants yet, if he would behave. Why this
question at this time, I wondered. She and my grandfather
took me everywhere, she claimed, and I was a
perfect little gentleman. At two years of age! And now,
thirty-eight years later I'm falling into a rage.
And I could see my grandfather's hard stare, his fixed
    expression
at the dinner table, and I thought how horrible, how monstrous
it was, to inflict *such manners* on a child of that age,
to make such an issue and priority out of it.
My grandfather had a stupendous capacity for rage
as well as a stern gaze. And backed it up with an imposing
physical presence. He was 6 ft tall and just about that wide.
His nickname was "Tarzan." When he rapped me on the
    knuckles
if I had the fork in my right hand I—must have—obeyed.
My mother obeyed too. How proudly he told of his travels
through Europe with his son before WWII: they'd enter
a bar or a hotel known to be closed off to Jews; and when
they so much as overheard some anti-Semitic comments
they'd beat the perpetrators into a "bloody pulp."
Or as a boy he would pitch steaming fastballs all afternoon

at his brother and when he saw the pain on his face
it made him pitch harder. THIS IS THE MAN WHO
    TAUGHT ME MANNERS!
By the time I wanted to call my friend the light had gone
    down,
it was dark in the barn, I could not see the numbers on
the phone to dial, Sam was still happily tying and untying
    himself,
the horses were snorting.

Nancy Schoenberger

MY GRANDMOTHER'S QUILT

It's not so much the "garment of contentment"
she pieced for herself, but an old quilt
that tells the world's story in random fabrics:
here's Noah's ark, aloft on a cotton flood,

the two by two of cambric animals
snipped from the stained tablecloth
and made part of the story. The creweled borders?
Blue waves of the deluge, God's wrath.

Let the dominant yellow patches stand for Ruth
in the alien corn, for blonde fields
where we stood, homesick and drowning,
in every state of the Union. Here's Egypt,

these chains of stitches where slaves wept
over the shaved heads of their women.
Now we come to Caesar's things: coins, medallions—
pieces of silk from mother's party dresses.

Scattered throughout are white cotton triangles,
butterflies, really—the resurrection
and the New World—pristine, innocent,
a little something for contentment.

The whole thing is moth-eaten (hordes
of locusts), leaving gaps in the tale,
primal O's where the wind blows through
and the threads of the story are lost, broken . . .

not a memento but a history in miniature
from my verse-quoting grandmother,
whose own girlhood stories
were buried with her.

E d w a r d   H i r s c h

ANCIENT SIGNS

In Memory of Oscar Ginsburg, 1894–1958

He loved statues with broken noses,
  the flaking white bodies of birches
after disease had set in,
        the memory of peasants
        kneeling at garish, hand-carved altars.

He loved old women washing laundry
  by the river, coolly slapping the
bedsheets senseless on the stones.
        It was sixty years later
        and yet he still couldn't forget them.

And he was still ashamed of the damp
  bodies of men's shirts filling the wind,
flapping about like chickens
        at the signs of hard weather.
        Only a woman's hands could calm them.

My grandfather loved thunderstorms.
  He loved to see the restless weaving
of trees and all the small shrubs
        kneeling down like penitents.
        As a child, in southern Latvia,

he used to run through the streets shouting
  while the ominous clouds moved slowly
across the dark horizon
        like a large foreign army
        coming to liberate the village.

My grandfather used to stand calmly
by the open window during storms.
He said that he could see lightning
            searching the empty rooftops,
        rifling the windows for his body.

He said that rain is an ancient sign
of the sky's sadness. And he said
that he could feel the wind trying
            to lift him into its arms,
        trying to carry him home again.

Carolyn Forché

THE MORNING BAKING

Grandma, come back, I forgot
How much lard for these rolls

Think you can put yourself in the ground
Like plain potatoes and grow in Ohio?
I am damn sick of getting fat like you

Think you can lie through your Slovak?
Tell filthy stories about the blood sausage?
Pish-pish nights at the virgin in Detroit?

I blame your raising me up for my Slav tongue
You beat me up out back, taught me to dance

I'll tell you I don't remember any kind of bread
Your wavy loaves of flesh
Stink through my sleep
The stars on your silk robes

But I'm glad I'll look when I'm old
Like a gypsy dusha hauling milk

Nicholas Christopher

ELEGY FOR
MY GRANDMOTHER

Now you're in the place where the shadows fly,
light-years away from this palm forest—
the room I've taken overlooking the Caribbean,
macaws squawking at the stars
and coconuts thudding to earth.

At your old house the garden lies barren;
lightning split the cherry trees,
black vines choked the azaleas.
You were famous for your green thumb.
Neighbors brought you their ailing plants,
and after a week on your terrace
the puniest amaryllis turned prodigy.
Your bags were always packed:
you loved to travel first-class, to sail
south at the earliest sign of winter.
I have a photograph of you in prewar Havana
wearing a white coat and feathered hat
after a day at the races,
gazing to sea (these same flashing waters)
from the casino balcony.
I remember you were cursed
with eyesight so sharp it daggered
migraines through your temples.
Once, driving in the country, you glanced
at a distant forest—
a blue band across the hills—
and counted the crows on a single bough.

You were first onto the dance floor
when the music started—and last to sit.

Before I could read, you taught me
poems and riddles, and those intricate
parables with the quirky endings—
your own variations on some theme.
You knew the real theme is always death,
and when I was ten you explained it to me:
one is on an enormous ship
(lush gardens lining the decks)
gliding over a white sea that never ends.
There is no horizon, no sun or moon:
the air is purest light.
The portholes are mirrors,
full of glittering expanses.
Somewhere on board an orchestra
is playing beautiful music,
but no one can find the musicians. . . .

Now that you're a passenger on that ship,
sailing and sailing into the light,
are they playing for you
on a dance floor strewn with flowers,
and is the music really so beautiful?
Nana, this was your way of telling me
you would never come back.

James Galvin

THE LAST MAN'S CLUB

My grandfather was always sad.
Sadly, as a boy, he paddled his canoe
along the beautiful Hudson River,
which was only then beginning to die.
During the first war
he was very sad in France because
he knew he was having the time of his life.
When it was over
everyone in America felt like a hero—imagine.
Once a year on Armistice Day,
he met with all his friends from the war.
They got drunk and recounted the stories
of the time when they had thought they were men
and the world had seemed entirely possible.
They placed empty chairs for certain of the dead,
and in the center of the table,
a bottle of cognac from France
for the last man of them to drink alone
in honor of the others.
Year after year they gathered to watch
each other and themselves disappear,
turn into empty chairs.
Sooner or later they all were sad.
Some of them must have realized
they didn't need to join a club for this.
Finally it was down to my grandfather
and a man named Oscar Cooper.
Neither one of them wanted to outlive anyone.
They couldn't remember what honor was.
When they drank the cognac
it didn't taste like anything.
They threw the bottle in the river

as if they thought it meant
that neither of them had to live anymore.
When Cooper died the following year,
my grandfather took his rifle out into the yard
and fired three shots at the sky.
Then he went down to the river
and drank himself to sleep.
After that he was never sad,
not even when the river died.

Garrett Kaoru Hongo

ISSEI: FIRST-GENERATION JAPANESE AMERICAN

An old man turning pages of books
Left to right. He reads backwards,
Up and down, *kanji* and *kana* script,
Over and over again. He does not see
The old words any more. The meanings
Lost, he pauses on a page and curls
His fingers, surrounding one lone
Character in the cradle of his hand.
He turns, knowing that I watch him
And pity the sleep in his eyes.
This is your name, he says,
We take it from son of prince.
Kaoru is your name.

David   Mura

GRANDFATHER   AND
GRANDMOTHER   IN   LOVE

Now I will ask for one true word beyond
betrayal, that creaks and buoys like the bedsprings
used by the bodies that begot the bodies that begot me.
Now I will think of the moon bluing the white
sheets soaked in sweat, that heard him whisper
haiku of clover, azalea, the cry of the cuckoo;
complaints of moles and beetles,
blight and bad debts, as the *biwa*'s spirit
bubbled up between them, its song quavering.
Now I take this word, crack it, like a seed
between the teeth, spit it out in the world
to root in the loam of his greenhouse roses;
let it leave the sweet taste of *teriyaki,*
a grain of her rice lodged in my molars;
in my nostrils, a faint hot breath of *sake.*

Now as *otoo-san, okaa-san,* drift towards
each other, there reverberates the *ran*
of lovers, and the ship of the past bursts
into that other world; and she, still teasing,
pushes him away, swats his hand, a pesky,
tickling fly, then turns to his face that
cries out laughing, as he hauls her in,
trawling the currents, gathering
a sea that seems endless, depths a boy dreams of,
where flounder, dolphin, fluorescent fins, fish
with wings spill before him glittering scales,
and letting slip the net, he dives under,
and night washes over them, slipping from
sight, just the soft shush of waves, drifting ground
swells, echoing the knocking tide of morning.

MI ABUELO

Where my grandfather is is in the ground
where you can hear the future
like an Indian with his ear at the tracks.
A pipe leads down to him so that sometimes
he whispers what will happen to a man
in town or how he will meet the best
dressed woman tomorrow and how the best
man at her wedding will chew the ground
next to her. Mi abuelo is the man
who speaks through all the mouths in my house.
An echo of me hitting the pipe sometimes
to stop him from saying *my hair is a*
sieve is the only other sound. It is a phrase
that among all others is the best,
he says, and *my hair is a sieve* is sometimes
repeated for hours out of the ground
when I let him, which is not often.
An abuelo should be much more than a man
like you! He stops then, and speaks: *I am a man*
who has served ants with the attitude
of a waiter, who has made each smile as only
an ant who is fat can, and they liked me best,
but there is nothing left. Yet I know he ground
green coffee beans as a child, and sometimes
he will talk about his wife, and sometimes
about when he was deaf and a man
cured him by mail and he heard groundhogs
talking, or about how he walked with a cane
he chewed on when he got hungry.
At best, mi abuelo is a liar.
I see an old picture of him at nani's with an
off-white yellow center mustache and sometimes

that's all I know for sure. He talks best
about these hills, *slowest waves,* and where this man
is going, and I'm convinced his hair is a sieve,
that his fever is cooled now underground.
Mi abuelo is an ordinary man.
I look down the pipe, sometimes, and see a
ripple-topped stream in its best suit, in the ground.

R i t a   D o v e

SUNDAY NIGHT AT GRANDFATHER'S

He liked to joke and all of his jokes were practical.
The bent thumb jiggling between two ribs, his
Faked and drunken swoon. We tipped by and
He caught us, grandfather's right, right
Up to the cliff of his pure white
Shirt, real Fruit-of-the-
Loom. We shrieked and
He cackled like
A living
Ghost.

He hated Billy the parakeet, mean as half-baked sin.
He hated church-going women and the radio turned
Up loud. His favorite son, called Billy
Too, had flown the coop although
Each year he visited, each
Time from a different
City, gold
Tooth and
Drunk.

Then out came the cherry soda and potato chips and pretzels.
Grandma humming hymns and rocking in the back bedroom.
Dad holding Billy out on a thick and bitten finger,
Saying *Here: Come on Joe—touch him.*
Every Sunday night the same.
Dad's quiet urging and
That laugh: *You've*
Got to be
Kidding,
Son.

Jimmy Santiago Baca

GREEN CHILE

I prefer red chile over my eggs
and potatoes for breakfast.
Red chile *ristras* decorate my door,
dry on my roof, and hang from eaves.
They lend open-air vegetable stands
historical grandeur, and gently swing
with an air of festive welcome.
I can hear them talking in the wind,
haggard, yellowing, crisp, rasping
tongues of old men, licking the breeze.

        But grandmother loves green chile.
When I visit her,
she holds the green chile pepper
in her wrinkled hands.
Ah, voluptuous, masculine,
an air of authority and youth simmers
from its swan-neck stem, tapering to a flowery
collar, fermenting resinous spice.
A well-dressed gentleman at the door
my grandmother takes sensuously in her hand,
rubbing its firm glossed sides,
caressing the oily rubbery serpent,
with mouth-watering fulfillment,
fondling its curves with gentle fingers.
Its bearing magnificent and taut
as flanks of a tiger in mid-leap,
she thrusts her blade into
and cuts it open, with lust

on her hot mouth, sweating over the stove,
bandanna round her forehead,

mysterious passion on her face
as she serves me green chile con carne
between soft warm leaves of corn tortillas,
with beans and rice—her sacrifice
to her little prince.
I slurp from my plate
with last bit of tortilla, my mouth burns
and I hiss and drink a tall glass of cold water.

All over New Mexico, sunburned men and women
drive rickety trucks stuffed with gunny-sacks
of green chile, from Belen, Veguita, Willard, Estancia,
San Antonio y Socorro, from fields
to roadside stands, you see them roasting green chile
in screen-sided homemade barrels, and for a dollar a bag,
we relive this old, beautiful ritual again and again.

Alice Fulton

PLUMBLINE

In memoriam: John Callahan, my grandfather

The world could snore, wrangle, or tear
itself to atoms while Papa sat
unnettled, bashful, his brain
a lathe smoothing thoughts civil
above fingers laced and pink

as baby booties; Papa, who said of any gambler,
roughneck, drunkard, just "I don't think much
of him," and in stiff denims
toted his lunchpail's spuds
down a plumbline of twelve-hour shifts:

farmed, lumbered, and cow-kicked,
let the bones knit their own
rivet, oiled big wheels that bullied
water uphill, drank stout, touched animals only
unawkwardly, drove four-in-hand, and sired six,

My ideas are dumb: a fizz
mute and thick as the head on a beer
he once thought, who never thought
such clabber could whiz through
genes and seed and speak.

Kate Daniels

GRANDMOTHER,
I'M READING TOLSTOY

In the long nights up north,
I've been reading Tolstoy and marveling
at how he knew what everyone
was thinking and even how they felt.
So many people inside him!
A whole city growing and sleeping
and being born. He was a kind master,
knowing exactly what everyone wanted
and loving them for it, no matter what.

I can't begin to imagine how you feel.

In the world I live in it's hard enough
to know *I* hurt when a man on the street
strokes my thigh with his long finger,
or that I marvel at the one-legged woman
hopping and pushing her bike through the park.

You've become something like a golden haystack
so big I couldn't gather it in my arms
if I tried.

I suppose I would like to know
you think it was worth it.

The sunsets up here are unusually painful
this time of year
as if someone raked his fingernails
through a delicate membrane.
I am reading Tolstoy and trying
to understand why you would want to die.

It's a world. All we can do is live
in it. I don't know. It's hard
to share your perspective.
You're at the end of the book.
I haven't gotten very far.
For me, it's still an accomplishment
just to turn over a page.

Tom Sleigh

LAST WISH

for my grandmother

The cars flashed like scales as the hearse-headed snake
Crawled down the dusty lane to the funeral tent
Flapping dove-gray wings in the wind-stropped heat.
I saw you snug in the hearse's air-conditioned gut

And imagined your eyes opening, peering
Through the cloud of velvet lining the brass lid,
Your thunder-gray pupils laconically resigned:
Dead or alive, your shrug, half-humorous, meant

More than your dull kiss: Frail as a baby bird,
Bald head swaddled in a red bandanna,
You craned forward, bared your gums, the words slurring
Round your exasperated, morphine-crippled tongue:

"Make sure they read Ecclesiastes,
 'Vanity, saith the preacher, all is vanity.'
 What your granddad didn't waste getting cross-eyed drunk
 I've squandered on the library. I know more folks

"In the graveyard than I do today in town."
 Your skull shone like a parable too simple
 To understand as you licked your blistered lips
 And motioned for the ice chips I fed you from

A spoon, your eyes, sly and daring, risking mine:
"Don't overdo it with the tears and such.
 I've left you your granddad's broken pocket-watch,
 The Santa Fe Special with the gold-plate back?

"Remember the seashells in the box upstairs
  And you can take your pick of the photographs.
  And do what your granddad said the day before he died,
  'Go out and get yourself a girl as good as mine.'

"Now there was a man who had no use for books——."
  And shrugging off the flush tinging your gray cheek:
"But what he lacked in brains he made up in looks."
  And staring straight through me: "You ought to write a poem."

Francisco Alarcón

IN A NEIGHBORHOOD
IN LOS ANGELES

I learned
Spanish
from my grandma

mijito
don't cry
she'd tell me

on the mornings
my parents
would leave

to work
at the fish
canneries

my grandma
would chat
with chairs

sing them
old
songs

dance
waltzes with them
in the kitchen

when she'd say
niño barrigón
she'd laugh

with my grandma
I learned
to count clouds

to point out
in flowerpots
mint leaves

my grandma
wore moons
on her dress

Mexico's mountains
deserts
ocean

in her eyes
I'd see them
in her braids

I'd touch them
in her voice
smell them

one day
I was told:
she went far away

but still
I feel her
with me

whispering
in my ear
mijito

Louise Erdrich

TURTLE MOUNTAIN RESERVATION

for Pat Gourneau, my grandfather

The heron makes a cross
flying low over the marsh.
Its heart is an old compass
pointing off in four directions.
It drags the world along,
the world it becomes.

My face surfaces in the green
beveled glass above the washstand.
My handprint in thick black powder
on the bedroom shade.
Home I could drink like thin fire
that gathers
like lead in my veins,
heart's armor, the coffee stains.

In the dust of the double hollyhock,
Theresa, one frail flame eating wind.
One slim candle
that snaps in the dry grass.
Ascending tall ladders
that walk to the edge of dusk.
Riding a blue cricket
through the tumult of the falling dawn.

At dusk the gray owl walks the length of the roof,
sharpening its talons on the shingles.
Grandpa leans back
between spoonfuls of canned soup
and repeats to himself a word

that belongs to a world
no one else can remember.

The day has not come
when from sloughs, the great salamander
lumbers through snow, salt, and fire
to be with him, throws the hatchet
of its head through the door of the three-room house
and eats the blue roses that are peeling off the walls.

Uncle Ray, drunk for three days
behind the jagged window
of a new government box,
drapes himself in fallen curtains, and dreams that the odd
beast seen near Cannonball, North Dakota,
crouches moaning at the door to his body. The latch
is the small hook and eye.

of religion. Twenty nuns
fall through clouds to park their butts
on the metal hasp. Surely that
would be considered miraculous almost anyplace,

but here in the Turtle Mountains
it is no more than common fact.
Raymond wakes,
but he can't shrug them off. He is looking up
dark tunnels of their sleeves,
and into their frozen armpits,
or is it heaven? He counts the points
of their hairs like stars.

One by one they blink out,
and Theresa comes forth
clothed in the lovely hair
she has been washing all day. She smells
like a hayfield, drifting pollen

of birch trees.
Her hair steals across her shoulders
like a postcard sunset.

All the boys tonight, goaded from below,
will approach her in The Blazer, The Tomahawk,
The White Roach Bar where everyone
gets up to cut the rug, wagging everything they got,
as the one bass drum of The Holy Greaseballs
lights a depth
charge through the smoke.

Grandpa leans closer to the bingo.
The small fortune his heart pumps for
is hidden in the stained, dancing numbers.
The Ping-Pong balls rise through colored lights,
brief as sparrows
God is in the sleight of the woman's hand.

He walks from Saint Ann's, limp and crazy
as the loon that calls its children
across the lake
in its broke, knowing laughter.
Hitchhiking home from the Mission, if he sings,
it is a loud, rasping wail
that saws through the spine
of Ira Comes Last, at the wheel.

Drawn up through the neck ropes,
drawn out of his stomach
by the spirit of the stones that line
the road and speak
to him only in their old agreement.
Ira knows the old man is nuts.
Lets him out at the road that leads up
over stars and the skulls of white cranes.

And through the soft explosions of cattail
and the scattering of seeds on still water,
walks Grandpa, all the time that there is in his hands
that have grown to be the twisted doubles
of the burrows of mole and badger,
that have come to be the absence
of birds in a nest.
Hands of earth, of this clay
I'm also made from.

KING SNAKE

Sometimes, my father's young life would resemble
something you'd hear in a Muddy Waters song.

Like the time he found out that the local hospitals would
pay good money for rattlesnakes in order to make anti-venom.

Soon he had a pen full, and I want to imagine my non-
body, his yet-to-be, whispering *careful* in his ear as he seeks
out his dangerous two-bits, but he's young, and reckless,
and I know how he gets when he sees a way to grab a buck.

I suppose his name gets around West Florida, because
one day, a white man drives up to the house, and makes a
better offer: One dollar a snake.

Of course he takes it, but when the white man who was
only paying my father fifty cents shows up, he doesn't take
kindly to the new arrangement. He curses my daddy out,
and threatens to return with the law.

This is a story my father thinks is no big deal, really,
just the daily stuff he had to do to live down there, and I
can see he's wondering why I want to make something of it.

But when the white man comes back, hauling with him
the sheriff, he gives me a description of my grandfather, a
black man with a long, handle-bar mustache who owns his
land, and holds a certain reputation.

When angered, we both stammer; unlike me, no one
cares to get him to that point.

This is proven by the way my father says the sheriff
decides to handle the situation.

When the car pulls up, my grandfather stands in the
front door. Tall? Stout? With Indian blood? No matter; he's
a quiet black man, on his own land, in the South in the late
twenties or early thirties, holding a shotgun. Holding a shot-
gun and saying nothing else.

My father can never tell me what my grandfather did to

earn this moment, what crazy, selfless or fearful things which came before that would lead the sheriff to side against the wounded pride of a white southern man.

And I want to yell, as wind blowing dust across the front yard, *watch your step* into their ears, but they both know more than I do, that nothing's going to happen, that they're all going to let the poor, silly man yell until his face turns red, and he simply runs out of breath and insults. My daddy will never be able to tell me what it was about my grandfather that tells the sheriff this just ain't worth the dance, or what it is in my sister that recalls my granddad to the relatives who knew him.

When my daddy was a young boy, he played with rattlesnakes. Can't you just hear Muddy Waters and Little Walter juking that out?

So baby, I sure know how to handle you.

Cathy Song

BLUE LANTERN

The blue lantern light
was like a full moon
swelling above the hush
of the mock orange shrubs
that separated our houses.

It was light
from your grandfather's room.

I remember the music
at night.

I dreamed the music
came in squares,
like birthday chocolate,
through the window
on a blue plate.

From his shakuhachi,
shavings of notes,
floated, and fell;
melted where the stillness
inserted itself back into night.
It was quiet then until dawn,
broken once by a single wailing:
the sound of an animal
whose hind leg is caught in a trap.

It was your grandfather
mourning his dead wife.
He played for her each night;
her absence,

the shape of his grief
funneled through the bamboo flute.
A ritual of remembrance,
keeping her memory alive
with his old breath.
He played unknowingly
to the child next door
who lay stricken by the music
transposed to her body,
waiting for the cry
that always surprised her;
like a glimpse of shadow
darting through the room
before she would drift off into sleep.

This was something we shared.
Listening, my eyes closed
as though I were under water
in the blueness of my room;
I felt buoyant and protected.

I imagined you, his grandson,
listening and lying
in your small bed;
your head making a slight
dent in the pillow.

It was as though the weight
of his grief washed over
the two of us
each night like a tide,
leaving our bodies beached
but unbruised,
white and firm like shells.

Li-Young Lee

I ASK MY MOTHER TO SING

She begins, and my grandmother joins her.
Mother and daughter sing like young girls.
If my father were alive, he would play
his accordion and sway like a boat.

I've never been in Peking, or the Summer Palace,
nor stood on the great Stone Boat to watch
the rain begin on Kuen Ming Lake, the picnickers
running away in the grass.

But I love to hear it sung;
how the waterlilies fill with rain until
they overturn, spilling water into water,
then rock back, and fill with more.

Both women have begun to cry.
But neither stops her song.

Permissions

1988 by Len Roberts. Reprinted by permission of Milkweed
Editions.

Rudman, Mark: "Manners" is reprinted by permission of the author.

Schoenberger, Nancy: "My Grandmother's Quilt" is from *Girl on a
White Porch: Poems*. Copyright © 1987 by Nancy Schoenberger. Re-
printed by permission of the University of Missouri Press.

Schultz, Philip: "Ode" is from *Deep Within the Ravine: Poems*. Copyright
© 1980 by Philip Shultz. Reprinted by permission of Viking
Penguin, a division of Penguin Books USA, Inc.

Shange, Ntozake: "Tango" is from *Nappy Edges*. Copyright © 1972,
1974, 1975, 1976, 1977, 1978 by Ntozake Shange and St. Martin's
Press, Inc. New York. Reprinted by permission.

Shapiro, Karl: "My Grandmother" is from *Collected Poems of Karl Shapiro
1940–1978* published by Random House, Inc. Copyright © 1978 by
Karl Shapiro. Reprinted by arrangement with Weiser & Weiser,
New York.

Simpson, Louis: "A Story About Chicken Soup" is from *At the End
of the Open Road*. Copyright © 1963 by Louis Simpson. Reprinted by
permission of Wesleyan University Press.

Sleigh, Tom: "Last Wish" is reprinted by permission of the author.

Smith, Bruce: "Incunabulum: With Grandmother at Nuzzie's" is re-
printed from *The Common Wages: Poems*. Copyright © 1983 by Bruce
Smith. Reprinted by permission of The Sheep Meadow Press.

Song, Cathy: "Blue Lantern" is from *Picture Bride* published by Yale Uni-
versity Press. Copyright © 1983 by Cathy Song. Reprinted by
permission.

Stafford, William: "One Day" is reprinted by permission of The Estate
of William Stafford.

Tate, James: "Summer Night" is from *Distance from Loved Ones* published
by Wesleyan University Press. Copyright © 1983 by James Tate.
Reprinted by permission of the University Press of New England.

Troupe, Quincy: "The Old People Speak of Death" is from *Weather
Reports: New & Selected Poems*. Copyright © 1991 by Quincy Troupe.
Reprinted by permission of Harlem River Press.

Valentine, Jean: "My Grandmother's Watch" is from *Home, Deep, Blue:
New and Selected Poems*. Copyright © 1988 by Jean Valentine. Re-
printed by permission of the author.

Van Doren, Mark: "Sleep, Grandmother" is from *The Collected and New
Poems of Mark Van Doren, 1924–1963*. Copyright © 1963 by Mark

About the Editor

Jason Shinder is author of the recent poetry collection,
Every Room We Ever Slept In, and editor of three previous volumes
in this anthology series. His forthcoming books include
Screen Gems, an anthology of movie poems, and *Faith*, a book-
length poem. He is founder of the The Writer's Voice of
the West Side YMCA in New York City and founder and executive
director of The National Writer's Voice Project of the YMCA
of the USA. Shinder presently teaches poetry writing at
Hunter College and The New School for Social Research
and divides his time between New York City and
Provincetown, Massachusetts.